A Chicago Tradition
Marshall Field's Food and Fashion

Joan Greene

Pomegranate

San Francisco

Published by Pomegranate Communications, Inc.

Box 808022, Petaluma CA 94975

800 227 1428; www.pomegranate.com

Pomegranate Europe Ltd.

Unit 1, Heathcote Business Centre

Hurlbutt Road, Warwick

Warwickshire CV34 6TD, UK

[+44] 0 1926 430111; sales@pomeurope.co.uk

Library of Congress Control Number: 2005903914

Pomegranate catalog no. A100

Cover and book design by Curtis Boyer

Printed in Korea

14 13 12 11 10 09 08 07 06 05   10 9 8 7 6 5 4 3 2 1

THE CHICAGO CULTURAL CENTER

Each year the Chicago Department of Cultural Affairs sponsors over 1,000 free programs designed to enrich the lives of people of all ages from all walks of life. Housed in a landmark building that was the Chicago Public Library and situated on Michigan Avenue between Washington and Randolph Streets, the Chicago Cultural Center is home to the world's largest Tiffany dome. Known as the People's Palace, the Center is the nation's first free municipal cultural center, one of the city's ten top attractions, and one of the most comprehensive free arts showcases in America.

Under the direction of Commissioner Lois Weisberg, the Chicago Department of Cultural Affairs is dedicated to serving the people of Chicago and visitors from around the globe by nurturing, enhancing, complementing, and marketing Chicago's cultural resources.

The Center houses seven exhibition spaces, three music stages, two theaters, a dance studio, a senior citizen center, a retail store, and the city's official visitor information center. Programming varies from Cultural Grants for neighborhood cultural and arts programming to Gallery 37, an internationally recognized program providing youth with apprenticeships with professional artists, to the World Kitchen Culinary Arts Programs.

Visit the Chicago Cultural Center at

78 E. Washington Street
Chicago IL 60602
312-744-6630

To my mother, Clyde Dean Greene, who taught my sister and me how to shop in the finest shops. To me, my mother is the fashion plate of our little town. My interest in Marshall Field's started with the stories that my best friend, Etta Foran, told me about going to the Walnut Room for Christmas with her mother and sitting under that Great Tree. This book is for Beatrice Tiernan, too.

ACKNOWLEDGEMENTS

Thank you to Lois Weisberg, Commissioner of Cultural Affairs, Chicago Department of Cultural Affairs, for believing in this project. Thanks to Katie Burke, Eva Strock, and Lisa Reid at Pomegranate and to Curtis Boyer. Many thanks to the great folks at Marshall Field's, Amy Meadows, Andrea Schwartz, Jamie Becker, Jeffrey Cassell, Donna Drolet, Chef Roger Coons, and the staff in the Walnut Room. Thank you, Tony Jahn, from Target Corporation. Tom Shroeder and Doris Burkland at Field Enterprises were a big help. At the Chicago Historical Society, thanks to Rob Medina; at the Harold Washington Library, Glenn Humphreys and Teresa Yoder deserve my appreciation. At the Cultural Affairs Center, much appreciation to Brad Thacker, Tim Samuelson, Ming Liu, and Eileen McCelligott.

And of course, a big thank-you to Marty and Amy Greene, Annette Crabtree, Jaime Harris, Etta Foran, Leslie Hindman, Mardi and Stan Timm, Stephanie Yaksic, Pilar Galvin, and Chuck Atkins.

1896 portrait of
Marshall Field, the
merchant prince.

Photograph courtesy Field Enterprises

INTRODUCTION

A visit to Chicago would not be complete without a trip to Marshall Field's on State Street. You begin with a walk under one of the big green landmark clocks at the corner of State and Randolph or State and Washington. Then take a turn through the brass revolving door and you are in the Mecca of shopping. The store has weathered destruction by fire not once but twice, the Civil War and two world wars, and the Great Depression, becoming an emblem of the city of Chicago and the standard by which retail is measured—or should be measured.

Marshall Field's is a sentimental place where generations have gone for a day of fine shopping and, if time permits, lunch or tea in the Walnut Room. And year after year entire families make the pilgrimage to Field's for the holiday window display and viewing of the Great Tree. Marshall Field's is as much a symbol of Chicago as the Wrigley Building or the Chicago Cubs. It is a place of drama and history, coupled with a vitality that changes with each generation as it celebrates the fashions and trends of the time. It is more than a retail store; it is an institution that has made history for more than 150 years.

Take a look at Marshall Field and Company and you will discover how many of the services that we take for granted today got their start in Chicago in the mid-1800s. Marshall Field was the man who made it

Chicago Historical Society

Marshall Field's, corner of Washington and State Streets, 1900s.

acceptable for a lady to do her shopping unescorted. He opened the first tearoom in a retail store, set fixed prices, displayed his goods in the windows, and established the concept of focusing on the female customer.

BEGINNINGS

Field's is a department store renowned for the profusion and quality of its goods, its gracious ambience, and its superb customer service. Since its inception, the store had been more geared to genteel elegance than any retail establishment before it. Marshall Field's can claim to have been the "first" with many of the services that we expect today.

To Chicagoans, Marshall Field and Company is a civic prize and a symbol of the city at its best. In 1852, Potter Palmer opened P. Palmer, Dry Goods and Carpets on Lake Street. In 1856, Marshall Field, age 22, arrived in Chicago from Pittsfield, Massachusetts, with less than a dollar in his pocket. Nine years later, Field and partner Levi Leiter purchased Potter Palmer's successful retail business. During the first year, the sales volume of Field, Leiter and Company reached $8 million, with a profit of $300,000. In 1881, Marshall Field bought out his partner and named his store Marshall Field and Company.

The present Marshall Field's department store building was completed in 1907, the largest retail store in the world, with seventy-three acres of space on thirteen floors. Today nine floors are used for retail.

Before Palmer and Field, no lady could go to a downtown restaurant without a male escort. There were no beauty shops or tearooms for women

Chicago Public Library, Special Collections and Preservation Division

Display of women's and children's attire at Marshall Field's in the 1890s.

Display of fabrics at Field's in the 1890s. By the end of the nineteenth century, Marshall Field's was the largest US importer of lace and silk.

of the carriage set. Women from the best families did not buy groceries or go to the drugstore. Men made purchases for their wives in the dry goods store while helping themselves to some liquid "refreshment." But with the opening of Marshall Field's, a new era of retailing was born, which played an important role in emancipating women. Field's was more than a place to shop; here an unescorted woman was catered to and waited on. Few other retreats existed for women. In the beautiful store that Potter Palmer started and Marshall Field improved upon, ladies found an acceptable place in which to shop and dine. Today women of all ages shop at Field's, considered one of the best department stores in America.

Marshall Field certainly had a flair for retail. In a little book he kept notes on his customers' buying habits—their likes, dislikes, and even family tidbits. He understood the value of making his store pleasing to the ladies and so paid great attention to stylish goods and fancy displays. He was polite to customers and had a good memory for names and faces. Above all, he valued service. Legend has it that striding through the store one day, Field overheard one of his clerks arguing with a customer. "What are you doing?" demanded Field. "I'm settling a complaint," the clerk responded. "No, you're not," said Field, "give the lady what she wants." That phrase became the motto for the store and set the course for fine retail establishments to this day.

When Field and Leiter bought out Palmer and rented a palatial marble building on State Street, the Chicago newspapers described the grand opening as "A Dazzling Assemblage of Wealth, Beauty, and Fashion." The first floor was devoted to retail, complete with walnut counters, frescoed walls, and splendid gas lighting fixtures. The merchandise—rich silks, sable-trimmed cloaks, Persian cashmere shawls, handmade lace—was displayed in grand style. Customer satisfaction was the utmost concern.

Retail general manager Harry Gordon Selfridge was always bursting with ideas. He emphasized the merchandise displays with more lighting, tripled the number of telephones, and turned the basement into a "budget floor." The idea of the bargain basement was to offer the same service and quality of goods as on the upstairs floors, but at lower prices. This was a brand-new concept in retailing, a way to introduce a new type of buyer to the store. In the first week of operation the basement carried dress goods, housekeeping linens, underwear, hosiery, gloves, ribbons, and other items that had not sold as well in their various departments.

When Marshall Field died in 1906, John Shedd became the president of the company. He oversaw the completion and opening of the current Chicago store. Shedd was noted for giving the employees advice: "Honesty always, courtesy always, readiness to oblige the customer's wishes, always. Keep the store handsome and spectacular for the shopping crowds. Never place price labels in window displays. Quality always, in goods, and in manners."

THE TEAROOM

Before 1890 there were no full-service tearooms at any retail department store in the world. Marshall Field felt that the people came to shop, not to eat, but something happened in 1890 that made him change his mind. One day Mrs. Hering, a salesclerk in the millinery department, overheard two of her guests complaining that there was not a decent place to eat on State Street. Not wanting to lose a big sale, Hering changed the course of history by offering the women her lunch of chicken potpie (her grandmother's recipe). She set a simple table, and so pleased the two women that they offered to bring several more friends the next day if she would again make her delicious chicken pie. The next day she set up five tables in the back of the millinery department, and served lunch to the ladies and their friends. Selfridge related this event to Field, who was then convinced to open an eating establishment; today, Mrs. Hering's Chicken Pot Pie is one of the top-selling items on the menu.

The South Tea Room opened on April 14, 1890. On that first day fifty-six guests were served; within a year as many as 1,500 people per day were being accommodated. On opening day there were fifteen tables, eight waitresses, and four women in the kitchen. The menu offered corned beef hash, chicken pie, chicken salad, orange punch in an orange shell, and Field's Rose Punch ice cream with dressing. A single red rose was placed on each plate.

Some of the specialties were prepared by local cooks in their own kitchens and brought to the tearoom's kitchen hours before the hungry crowds would appear. In time, the Walnut Tearoom—as it came to be called—was one of several restaurants and dining rooms on the seventh floor of the State Street store (The Men's Grill room was on the sixth

Ladies who lunch, at Marshall Field's in the 1940s.

Chuck Atkins/Joan Greene Design Group, Inc.

MRS. HERING'S CHICKEN POT PIE

SERVES 4

3 teaspoons butter
¼ cup all-purpose flour
2 cups chicken broth
Salt and pepper to taste
12 oz cooked chicken breast, cubed
¼ cup frozen peas, thawed
¼ cup cooked carrot, diced
4 casserole dishes, each with
   1½- to 2-cup capacity
1 sheet puff pastry, thawed

1. *Melt butter in a large, heavy-bottomed pan.*
2. *Stir in flour and cook for 1 minute.*
3. *Add chicken broth, whisking until it reaches a boil; let cook for 2 minutes.*
4. *Season with salt and pepper.*
5. *Add chicken, peas, and carrots.*
6. *Divide filling into 4 casserole dishes.*
7. *Cut 4 circles from puff pastry and fit over the top of each casserole.*
8. *With a knife, cut two 1-inch slits in each pastry; tuck pastry under each side.*
9. *Cook in oven 22 to 27 minutes, until pastry is puffed up and golden brown.*

floor of a separate building in which The Store for Men was located). In the 1920s the Walnut Room menu noted that "on request, a page may be called who will locate friends in the Tea Room and Grill Rooms, also to deliver messages or arrange for telephone communication for you." There was no charge for the service. The fare and the presentation varied from restaurant to restaurant, from grilled chops and steaks to little sandwiches served in baskets with ribbon bows tied to the handles. Diners could select from the Narcissus Fountain Room—where tea was served from 3 to 5 in the afternoon—the Mission Grill Room, the Crystal Tea Room, the Colonial Tea Room (handy for diners wanting quick service), and the Wedgewood Room.

Over the years, Field's has added other restaurants. For a while, the Cloud Room at Midway Airport was second only to the Walnut Room in popularity. In the basement of the store today, a food court and the sports café/bar Infield's are favorite dining spots. On the seventh floor is the Frango Café, named in honor of the mints for which the store is famous. In 1929, Field's acquired the Frederick & Nelson Company of Seattle and their Franco Mints. In the 1930s, the name was changed to Frango to avoid similarity to Spanish dictator Francisco Franco's name. For many years the candy was actually made in-house at the State Street store, but in 1999 production was moved to the East Coast. Today, over 1 million pounds of Frango chocolates are sold throughout the store, and Frango Mint Chocolate Chip Cookies and Frango Mint Chocolate Cheesecake are favorite menu items.

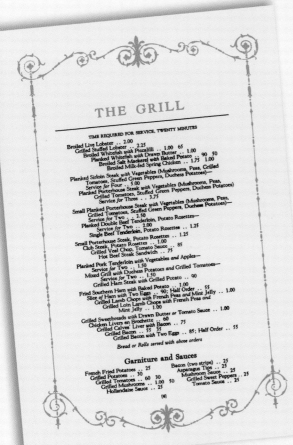

THE GRILL

TIME REQUIRED FOR SERVICE, TWENTY MINUTES

Broiled Live Lobster .. 2.00
Grilled Stuffed Lobster .. 2.25
    Broiled Whitefish with Piccalilli .. 1.00 65
      Planked Whitefish with Drawn Butter .. 1.00
      Broiled Salt Mackerel with Baked Potato .. 90 50
        Broiled Milk-fed Spring Chicken .. 1.75 1.00

Planked Sirloin Steak with Vegetables (Mushrooms, Peas, Grilled
    Tomatoes, Stuffed Green Peppers, Duchess Potatoes)—
      Service for Four .. 5.00
Planked Porterhouse Steak with Vegetables (Mushrooms, Peas,
    Grilled Tomatoes, Stuffed Green Peppers, Duchess Potatoes)
      Service for Three .. 3.75
Small Planked Porterhouse Steak with Vegetables (Mushrooms, Peas,
    Grilled Tomatoes, Stuffed Green Peppers, Duchess Potatoes)—
      Service for Two .. 2.50
Planked Double Beef Tenderloin, Potato Rosettes—
      Service for Two .. 2.00
    Single Beef Tenderloin, Potato Rosettes .. 1.25

Small Porterhouse Steak, Potato Rosettes .. 1.25
    Club Steak, Potato Rosettes .. 1.00
    Grilled Veal Chop, Tomato Sauce .. 85
      Hot Beef Steak Sandwich .. 75

Planked Pork Tenderloin with Vegetables and Apples—
    Service for Two .. 1.50
    Mixed Grill with Duchess Potatoes and Grilled Tomatoes—
      Service for Two .. 1.50
      Grilled Ham Steak with Grilled Potato .. 90

Fried Southern Ham with Baked Potato .. 1.00
    Slice of Ham with Two Eggs .. 90; Half Order .. 55
      Grilled Lamb Chops with French Peas and Mint Jelly .. 1.00
        Grilled Loin Lamb Chops with French Peas and
        Mint Jelly .. 1.00

Grilled Sweetbreads with Drawn Butter or Tomato Sauce .. 1.00
    Chicken Livers en Brochette .. 60
      Grilled Calves' Liver with Bacon .. 75
      Grilled Bacon .. 55 35
        Grilled Bacon with Two Eggs .. 85; Half Order .. 55

Bread or Rolls served with above orders

Garniture and Sauces

French Fried Potatoes .. 25   Bacon (two strips) .. 25
Grilled Potatoes .. 30   Asparagus Tips .. 25
Grilled Tomatoes .. 60 30   Mushroom Sauce .. 25
Grilled Mushrooms .. 1.00 50   Grilled Sweet Peppers .. 25
Hollandaise Sauce .. 25   Tomato Sauce .. 25

[6]

A page from the Walnut Grill menu. By the late 1930s the South Tea Room was called the Walnut Room, after the Circassian walnut wood paneling on the walls. Today it is one of the oldest operating restaurants in Chicago.

The Narcissus Room—named for the Roman god topping the fountain in the room—was completed in 1914 and expanded across much of the seventh floor; it was almost a city block in size. The tearoom was a favorite place to relax; today the room is used for special functions and can be rented for private events. The mirror in this image reflects the interior of the Narcissus Room.

The architectural centerpiece of the Walnut Room—shown here in 1992—is a beautiful multistory rotunda adorned with Austrian crystal chandeliers, mounted French ceramics, and a one-story-high fountain.

On March 19, 1948, Field's opened a restaurant at Midway Airport, at the time the world's busiest airport. Airlines flew in souvenirs and delicacies from all over the world for the grand opening, including leis from Hawaii, orchids from Mexico, lobster from Africa, and strawberries from California.

The neighborhood pub called Infield's might be considered the modern-day Men's Grill. It is a great spot for lunch and for the latest news on the city's sports teams.

Photograph by Susan Kezon for Marshall Field's

The Frango Café on the seventh floor features chocolate cheesecake made with Frango mints (see recipe p. 23).

Marshall Field's Archives

21

FRANGO MINT CHOCOLATE CHIP COOKIES

Makes 8 dozen cookies; can be made up to 5 days in advance if stored in an airtight container.

Baking sheets
Parchment paper
2½ cups flour
1 teaspoon baking soda
½ teaspoon salt
½ cup (1 stick) unsalted butter at room
   temperature
½ cup solid vegetable shortening
1 cup firmly packed light brown sugar
½ cup granulated sugar
2 large eggs, at room temperature
5 Frango Mint Chocolates chopped
   very fine (should be ¼ cup)
1 teaspoon vanilla extract
25 Frango Mint Chocolates chopped
   coarse (about 1⅔ cups)
¾ cup chopped pecans

Preheat the oven to 350° F. Line two baking sheets with parchment paper, or use a nonstick baking sheet.

Sift together the flour, baking soda, and salt. With a handheld mixer set at medium speed, cream the butter and shortening together for about 1 minute; add the sugars and mix about another minute. Beat in the eggs, very finely chopped chocolates, and vanilla. Stir in the coarsely chopped chocolates and pecans until blended. Drop rounded teaspoons of the cookie dough about 1 inch apart on the prepared cookie sheets.

Bake until nearly firm but still soft in the center, for about 10 minutes. Transfer cookies to wire racks to cool. (Let the baking sheets cool down before reusing them.) Store the cookies in an airtight container at room temperature.

FRANGO MINT CHOCOLATE CHEESECAKE

Can be made up to 2 days in advance, if covered and refrigerated.

Crust

¾ cup graham cracker crumbs
4 tablespoons melted unsalted butter
1 tablespoon + 1 teaspoon sugar

Combine ingredients in a processor or mixer. Press mixture evenly and firmly into the bottom of an ungreased, 8-inch round, springform pan that is at least 2 inches deep.

Filling

15 Frango Mint (milk) chocolates
  chopped coarse
3 8-ounce packages cream cheese at
  room temperature
1 cup sugar
2 large eggs at room temperature
⅓ cup heavy (whipping) cream
½ teaspoon vanilla extract

Melt the chopped chocolates in a double boiler over hot (not boiling) water; stir frequently. Remove from heat and cool the chocolate until it is tepid.

In a large bowl, beat the cream cheese with an electric mixer at medium speed, until it is smooth. Add sugar and blend well, Add eggs, one at a time. Add the cooled chocolate, cream, and vanilla and beat until well mixed. Pour mixture into the crust.

Preheat oven to 350° F. Place crust on a rack in the center of the preheated oven. Bake crust until the sides rise and the top jiggles slightly when shaken (takes 35 to 40 minutes). The cake will look underbaked but will firm upon chilling. Run a sharp knife around the inside of the pan to release the cake from the sides of the pan. Cool the cake completely in the pan on a wire rack.

Topping

¼ teaspoon unflavored gelatin
1 tablespoon cold water
3 Frango Mint milk chocolates finely
  chopped
½ cup sour cream at room
  temperature

In a small bowl, soften the gelatin in the cold water. Transfer the gelatin to a double boiler; stir over hot water until the gelatin is dissolved. Add the chopped chocolate and stir until melted. Remove the pan from the heat and let the mixture cool until tepid. Whisk the sour cream and chocolate mixture together until blended. Spread the topping over the cooled cheesecake. Cover the cake with plastic wrap and refrigerate at least 4 hours. Remove the sides of the springform pan; smooth the sides of the cake with a wet, hot knife.

To serve, garnish with whipped cream and a sprig of fresh mint.

THE GREAT TREE

The centerpiece of every Marshall Field's holiday is the famous Great Tree in the Walnut Room, a cherished tradition since 1907, when the manager of the Walnut Room gave money to a busboy to find a tree with which to decorate the restaurant. By 1917 the Christmas tree had become such a popular tradition that Field's created an entire display division, the Tree Design Bureau, to handle the procuring, erecting, and decorating of the Great Tree.

The 45-foot-high tree welcomes over 25,000 people on busy days. The wait for breakfast, lunch, and dinner can be as long as three hours. The Great Tree turns the restaurant into an enchanted place. In 1962 fire codes forced Field's to use an artificial tree; supposedly, in 1963 two women waiting in line got a choice seat at the edge of the tree and one commented to the other that she could smell the pine. Under the tree at Field's is a magical spot.

Through the years, Field's has continued to cater to its customers' eating pleasure. Between 1918 and 1922 recipe cards were created to highlight the Household Utilities Department; they called for using items that Field's sold: strainer, measuring cup, omelet pan, waffle pan. Children are not overlooked at Field's: many favorites are prepared for the kids, including Field's Ice Cream Snowman Sundae, the most popular children's dessert. In 2003 the Walnut Room put a different ice cream dessert on the menu for Christmas—protests were loud and long. In 2004, the Snowman Sundae was back for the season.

In 2003 the Great Tree sparkled with crystal and fiber optics. Designer Jim O'Leary of Waterford Crystal, Ireland, beautifully blended tradition and innovation.

Photograph by Susan Kezon for Marshall Fields

FIELD'S ICE CREAM SNOWMAN SUNDAE

In a cold, frosted dessert dish place the following just before serving:

1 scoop vanilla ice cream for body

3 raisins for buttons (or use chocolate chips or dried cranberries)

1 marshmallow for head; with watered-down pure red food coloring, paint on
   eyes, nose, and mouth with a toothpick

½ maraschino cherry for snowman's red cap

2 red licorice twists for arms (or use candy canes or cookie sticks)

A 1952 children's lunch menu from one of Field's tearooms. It is interesting to note the change in food preferences over the years.

Marshall Field & Company

Children's Menu

CLOWN LUNCHEON
★Creamed chicken flakes in a whipped potato
nest, served with buttered carrots 90

ORGAN GRINDER'S LUNCHEON
(allow 15 minutes for cooking)
Scrambled egg and crisp bacon,
served with apple sauce 65

LITTLE RED HEN
Chicken croquette in a nest of fried noodles,
whipped potatoes with gravy,
buttered carrots with peas 75

BIG TENT (allow 15 minutes for broiling)
Chopped beef patty, creamed potatoes
and buttered peas 1.00

★A substitution for meat may be served on Friday upon request.

Choice of ice cream or
Fruit jello served with a sugar cookie

Milk or hot chocolate

(Children's portion of some items on regular menu
may be obtained)

Author's collection

READY TO SERVE

Mixed fruit salad with sandwiches 40
A cup of chicken broth with noodles 20

SANDWICHES

Minced chicken on homemade bread 30
Peanut butter with jelly 35
Sliced ham and lettuce 60
Whitemeat tunafish salad 50

DESSERTS

Rainbow ice cream cake roll 30
Dunce cap ice cream 25
Merry-go-round ice cream 25
King Cole ice cream 25

BEVERAGES

Pasteurized "Grade A" milk
with graham crackers 15
Purple cow 20
Black cow 20
Chocolate milk 15
Strawberry milk shake 25

An amount will be added to quoted prices of all foods to cover
additional expenses due to the Illinois Retailers Occupation Tax

All prices are our O.P.S. ceiling prices or lower. A list showing
our ceiling prices for each item is available for your inspection.

8-7-52   THIS IS YOURS TO TAKE HOME

CORNMEAL WAFFLES

In upper part of double boiler cook 1 cupful of white cornmeal with 2 cupfuls of boiling salted water for 20 minutes. After cooling slightly, add 2 well-beaten eggs and about 2½ cupfuls flour, sifted with 1 teaspoonful salt, 3 teaspoonfuls baking powder, and 3 tablespoonfuls sugar; 2 tablespoonfuls of melted butter, or butter substitute, and 1½ cupfuls of milk. Bake on hot waffle irons.

This recipe has been tested by the Girl in the Cap and Apron

Household Utilities Ninth Floor

MARSHALL FIELD & COMPANY

DUCHESS SOUP

4 cups white stock
2 slices carrots, cut in cubes
2 slices onion
2 blades mace
¼ cup grated mild cheese

¼ cup butter
¼ cup flour
¼ teaspoonful salt
2 cups scalded milk
⅛ teaspoonful pepper

Cook vegetables 3 minutes in 1½ tablespoonfuls of butter, then add stock and mace, boil 15 minutes, strain and add milk. Thicken with remaining butter and flour cooked together; add salt and pepper. Stir in cheese, and serve as soon as cheese is melted.

WHITE SOUP STOCK
The water (4 cups) in which chicken has been cooked.

This recipe has been tested by the Girl in the Cap and Apron

Household Utilities Ninth Floor

MARSHALL FIELD & COMPANY

POTATO SALAD

After paring the skins from the potatoes which have been boiled until tender, but not broken, dice and measure. To 1 quart of potatoes add 1 cup of cooked salad dressing which has been thinned with 1 cup of cream.

1 chopped onion
Salt, pepper, paprika

2 tablespoonfuls chopped parsley
¼ teaspoonful lemon essence and a bit of cinnamon and cloves.

Garnish with cooked eggs and parsley.

This recipe has been tested by the Girl in the Cap and Apron

Household Utilities Ninth Floor

MARSHALL FIELD & COMPANY

BRAZILIAN SHRIMPS

1 pound (or 1 can) shrimps
1 pint tomato juice
1 green pepper

1 onion
1 tablespoonful butter
2 tablespoonfuls flour

1 teaspoonful sugar

Cut the pepper and onion in strips and place them in a saucepan with the tomato juice. Let this boil about 15 minutes, and then add the shrimps. Blend the butter and flour together, and add this blend to the mixture. Allow the whole to boil together until it is smooth.

This recipe has been tested by the Girl in the Cap and Apron

Household Utilities Ninth Floor

MARSHALL FIELD & COMPANY

Between 1918 and 1922, free recipe cards were handed out in the housewares department, to encourage shoppers to buy the cooking equipment listed in the recipes.

Photograph courtesy Marshall Fields

The twelve-member Field's Culinary Council. These top chefs advise Field's and create new recipes.

Continuing its commitment to food, in fall 2003 the store introduced the Field's Culinary Council, an advisory committee composed originally of nine of the country's top chefs but now made up of twelve members: Rick Bayless, Elizabeth Brown, Tom Douglas, Tyler Florence, Gale Gand, Andrea Immer, Tim Scott, Nancy Silverton, Ming Tsai, Todd English, Marcus Samuelsson, and Takashi Yagihashi. Two of the newest chefs have already contributed recipes sure to become classics: Chef Gale Gand's Banana Maple Tarte Tatin and Chef Takashi Yagihashi's Spring Onion Soup.

The store has also set up the Field's Culinary Studio, where guests can take cooking classes, and fresh gourmet dishes are created for sale in the Marketplace on the lower level and served in the store's various restaurants.

CHEF GALE GAND'S BANANA MAPLE TARTE TATIN
SERVES 8

1 sheet frozen puff pastry, thawed
   overnight in the refrigerator
Flour
Rolling pin
Baking pan: heavyweight 9″ or 10″ cake
   pan or heavy, ovenproof, 10″ skillet
Sheet pan
2 tablespoons unsalted butter
½ cup pure maple syrup
1 whole vanilla bean, cut in half
   lengthwise
2–3 bananas, sliced into ½″-thick circles
Vanilla ice cream

Unfold pastry on a lightly floured work surface; lightly roll the rolling pin over it to smooth out creases and make the pastry a bit thinner. Using your baking pan as a guide, cut a round of dough no bigger than the pan all the way around. Transfer the circle of dough to the sheet pan; prick the dough with a fork, and keep it refrigerated.

Heat the oven to 425° F. Place the baking pan on the stove and add the butter. Turn heat to medium; heat butter until it is melted. Add the maple syrup and vanilla bean and bring the mixture to a boil, stirring occasionally. Turn off the heat; position the vanilla bean in the center of the baking pan. Cover the entire bottom of the pan with the banana slices.

Lay the pastry circle over the bananas, pressing the extra pastry around the sides of the pan so it comes up the wall of the pan rather than down the bananas. The pastry will shrink to fit the pan. Bake pastry 20–25 minutes, until it is golden brown. Let it cool in the pan for at least 30 minutes.

Just before serving, warm the bottom of the baking pan 1–2 minutes on the stove over low heat, to melt the caramel slightly and loosen the tart from the pan. Place a serving plate over the pan and quickly flip over both, to turn the tart out, with bananas facing up. Serve with vanilla ice cream, if desired.

CHEF TAKASHI YAGIHASHI'S SPRING ONION SOUP
SERVES 6

Onions

5 pounds spring onions, split in half
¼ cup olive oil
⅛ cup sugar

*Preheat oven to 400° F. In a roasting pan,
place the onions cut side up; drizzle olive oil
and sugar over the top of the onions. Place
pan in oven and let onions cook 1½ hours.*

Remove from oven and set aside.

Soup

½ cup olive oil
4 ounces slab bacon, chopped (optional)
½ pound white domestic mushrooms,
    chopped
½ pound parsnips, chopped
½ pound leeks, white part only, washed
    clean of all dirt
1½ ounces garlic, chopped
6 quarts chicken stock
½ tablespoon cumin
½ tablespoon Spanish paprika
½ tablespoon dark chili powder
1 ounce sherry vinegar
½ quart half & half or heavy cream
Salt, pepper

*Place a large sauté pan over medium heat;
add olive oil and bacon. Sauté bacon until it
is golden brown (about 5 minutes). Then
add mushrooms, parsnips, leeks, and garlic.
Continue sautéing for about 20 minutes,
stirring every 30 seconds to prevent burning.*

*Once vegetables are soft, add the reserved
spring onions and continue to sauté another
10 minutes. Add chicken stock and bring to a
boil; then bring back down to a simmer. Let
soup simmer 20 minutes on low heat, then
add the cumin, paprika, chili powder, and
vinegar; let it all simmer 5 more minutes.*

*Put soup in a blender and purée until very
smooth. Pass soup through a fine strainer
into a clean saucepan and season with salt
and pepper. Add the half & half or heavy
cream; bring up to boiling over medium heat.*

Salad garnish

6 asparagus spears, tender part only,
    cut into 2″ lengths
6 slices pancetta, sliced thin, 2″ wide,
    4″ long
1 cup fresh arugula, leaf only, julienned

*Roll three pieces of asparagus with the
pancetta to make six bundles. Grill the
asparagus over medium heat, 2 minutes on
each side, or until the pancetta is crispy
and the asparagus is cooked. Season with
salt and pepper.*

To serve

*Divide the arugula among six
bowls, about one tablespoon
per bowl. Place grilled
asparagus on top of the
arugula. Pour soup around
the garnish and serve immediately.*

As part of the emphasis on fresh and modern cuisine, Field's offers cooking demonstrations several times a day.

CUSTOMER SERVICE

Marshall Field's blazed the trail for retail service at its best. By 1890, Eddie Anderson, the greeter and doorman at the Washington Street entrance, was probably the country's first personal shopper; prominent Chicago families often called upon him to select a needed item, such as the right black coat for a funeral or a gift for a newborn. In 1893, as the World's Fair approached, Field's hired interpreters to help foreign shoppers get around the city and to make their experience at the store comfortable and enjoyable.

The strong demand for personal service led to the creation of a special unit to handle telephone calls. The women who handled phone requests were known as Personal Shoppers, and they provided that extra something for customers. For example, an Australian businessman contacted Field's for an entire new wardrobe for his wife. A Personal Shopper asked the man for his wife's measurements, a brief description of her social activities, and a photograph of her. By the time the man was ready to check out of his hotel, a complete wardrobe had been selected, packaged, and delivered to his room.

The department heads at Field's always knew the finest restaurants, the best shows, and the best ways to get around Chicago. Today a guest can get all sorts of information about the store and touring Chicago on the first floor, at Field's Express desk in the Atrium, or on the seventh floor, at the Visitor Center.

The concept of service flowed over into every aspect of the store's business. By the early 1900s there was even a branch of the Chicago public library located in Marshall Field's; it was the largest substation of the

Personal shopping operators at Marshall Field's, 1934. Calls came in from all over the world for that special, individual touch.

city's library, with a circulation of over 5,000 books per month. The library was beautifully appointed, with Oriental rugs and lush green leather and mahogany furniture.

Field's had such a strong reputation for service and fine goods that in 1896, when William McKinley won the presidency, his wife called on the fitters and dressmakers at Marshall Field's to create her inaugural gown— the president-elect came with her to the fitting. And supposedly, when Isadora Duncan came to Chicago from San Francisco looking for a job as a dancer, the manager of the Masonic Temple roof garden told her to get a frilly dress to go with her unusual style of dance. Duncan glided into Field's and asked to speak with the manager, Harry Selfridge. Selfridge could not help but smile when he met the avant-garde woman, and he told her that she could have anything she wanted. She carefully selected some white and red material for petticoats and some lace frills, pressed Selfridge's hand with gratitude, and went on to become a great dance sensation.

The women who stepped through the doors of Marshall Field and Company on opening day in 1907 set the pace for women today. By the beginning of the twentieth century, female customers were spending 80 percent of the consumer dollar. They were no longer helpless; they were healthier, better educated, more athletic, taller, stronger, and more self-assured than the women before them. Retailers were finally realizing that women's patronage was key, a concept that years earlier Marshall Field had intuitively understood.

DELIVERY SERVICE

Marshall Field started free horse and wagon delivery service in 1872. Field's advertised that its delivery men would "Be On Time. Be Correct. Deliver Neat Packages."

By 1913, Field's had 188 motor trucks for delivery, as well as 142 wagons and 375 horses. They would deliver to a 35-mile radius from the store.

By the 1960s Field's corps of deliverymen, trained as goodwill ambassadors, were more than 400 strong and made 25,000 deliveries a day from store-owned trucks painted a special green. A Field deliveryman would not have thought of barging right up a customer's step with a Christmas sled or bicycle. He knocked first with an empty hand. If the coast were clear, he went back to the truck for the gift; often he was requested to leave it with a neighbor. Field's deliverymen were so cherished that many stayed on the job for forty years.

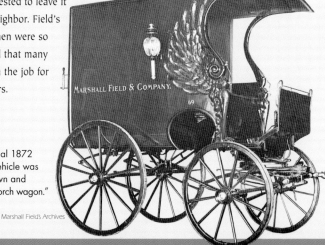

The original 1872 delivery vehicle was horse drawn and called a "torch wagon."

Marshall Field's Archives

Chicago Public Library, Special Collections, and Preservation Division

By the 1890s, many delivery carriages lined up each day for their morning run. In 2003, two London taxicabs became the store's newest delivery vehicles. If you live within 5 miles of the State Street store and buy something that you need help getting home, one of these neat little taxis will deliver.

Marshall Field's

Marshall Field's Archives

FASHION—BRINGING THE WORLD TO THE MIDWEST

Perhaps more than any other merchant, Marshall Field understood the great drama of retail sales: female oriented, beautiful window displays, merchandising rather than warehousing goods, and treating the customer as a valued client. The State Street store burned to the ground in the Fire of 1871, and again in 1877, but each time Field's reopened with a spectacular flourish. For a decade or so after the World's Fair of 1893, Marshall Field and Company imported nearly $3 million per year in foreign goods, its buyers combing the globe for fine, unique merchandise to bring back home. By 1895, Field's was the country's largest importer of laces. Field also held exclusive rights to import French gloves and was the wholesale agent for French gloves all across the country, at a time when no lady would be seen in public without gloves. As early as 1850, Field was the first American retailer to send style experts to Paris to learn the latest in fashion; in 1870 he established the first European buying office. And for many years, Field's hats were actually designed and created in a studio within the store.

In 1895, Arthur Valair Fraser, a window dresser from Creston, Iowa, came to the attention of Field's executives, who subsequently hired him. He forever changed how retail goods are displayed. Dry goods stores at the time put something of everything they had in the window, but Fraser believed that one great item told the story. Under Fraser, the windows at Marshall Field's became world famous and were the standard by which other retailers around the globe were judged.

Transplanting Paris

At a famous numero of the rue de la Paix, appraising eyes review passing creations . . . Somewhere on the rue St. Honoré a man who has bought millions of gloves for us selects several of the better new styles . . . One shrewd young man knows where to go in Paris for marvelous costume jewelry; another for hosiery more sheer than shadows; another for tapestries that few may own but none fail to admire. ● These are some of Marshall Field and Company's large staff of resident representatives in Paris. In addition, scores of men and women from Field's in Chicago visit Paris periodically. Alert, fashion-wise, their purchases reflect an intimate knowledge of Continental correctness. ● You are cordially invited to come to Field's for almost anything you might like from Paris.

Marshall Field and Company   RETAIL · CHICAGO

A page from a millinery booklet produced by Marshall Field and Company during the 1890s.

THE flower cockade is a skillful blending of the modish hues further carried out by the blue velvet on the fancy braid of cerise. $13.75

No. 410

ECRU braid, trimmed with royal blue ribbon, yellow-centered white daisies, and pink roses. $15.00

No. 418

Marshall Field's Archives

Famed window dresser Arthur Fraser felt that display windows should catch the viewer's eye with color and design and make the viewer think.

Marshall Field's Archives

Arthur Fraser had a staff of twenty display artists, painters, carpenters, and plaster molders. The 1920s window reveals the meticulous detail paid to the displays. By the 1940s, Fraser's legacy was still evident, even though his reign ended in 1944.

Marshall Field's Archives

43

In this 1902 photograph, ladies are viewing the finest fashions in the dress salon.

SEW IT YOURSELF
A COLORFUL FALL WARDROBE FROM OUR BLOCK OF FABRICS

Marshall Field's Archives

During the 1940s you could "Sew It Yourself" from fabric sold at Marshall Field's.

Main aisle display during Field's Spring Fashion Show, 2005.

BRIDAL

As far back as the 1890s, Marshall Field's was the in spot in the Midwest for a spectacular wedding gown and trousseau. It was said that Field himself would bring back beautiful handmade lace from Europe for a waiting bride in Chicago. In 1924, a wedding secretary service was created to advise brides-to-be; soon known as the Wedding Bureau, the service became the first bridal registry in the United States. During the 1920s, the Bride's Room was designed and set up solely for the bride's convenience. Here the bride could plan and select her entire trousseau as well as learn about wedding protocol, get information about honeymoon retreats, and find out how to care for and maintain a home.

Marshall Field's traditionally is a place where memories are made. Nowhere is that more evident than in the Bridal Salon. If you wind your way through the entrance to the bridal shop and head toward the fitting rooms and the bridesmaid gowns, you will come upon a poignant treasure. On June 27, 1936, Miss Rose Slupkowski wed Mr. Raymond Szpekowski. Rose and Raymond were not famous people, but Rose's beautiful size 0 silk wedding gown from Marshall Field's has a place of honor in the Bridal Salon.

Rose's daughter, a retired Field's employee, brought the gown, packed in its original box, to the store. The fact that Field's made room to display that lovely gown and the mementos from a wedding so long ago demonstrates Field's understanding that sometimes it is more important to honor tradition than to fill every square inch with sellable merchandise.

Chuck Atkins/Joan Greene Design Group, Inc.

Rose Slupkowski's Marshall Field's gown, her seamed silk stockings, and the groom's boutonnière from her 1936 wedding are on display in the Bridal Salon.

Chuck Atkins/Joan Greene Design Group, Inc.

Also on display at the entrance to the Bridal Salon is the paper gown created by Belgian artist and designer Isabelle de Borchgrave.

A bride being fitted for her gown at Marshall Field's, 1953.

FASHIONS OF THE HOUR

Marshall Field and Company began issuing its famous and unique *Fashions of the Hour* magazine in October 1914. The large-sized publication (about 13 x 9 1/2 inches) had color covers and presented a considerable amount of information for the shopper. Fashions ranged from thirty-two to forty or so pages; inside each issue were articles about local places of interest, Chicago social and cultural events, and other topics sure to attract the reader, such as gardening and the silver screen. Store events like previews, openings of new shops, exhibits, teas, and the annual Marshall Field's Choral Society musicals were also covered; an occasional poem would appear. Photographs of Hollywood stars and Chicago socialites captured them wearing Field's versions of notable Parisian and American fashions. Liberally scattered throughout the pages were abundant drawings of the clothing and accessories offered for sale at Marshall Field's in what seemed to be a limitless number of departments, including the French Dressmaking Rooms and The Store for Men: hats, sportswear, perfumes, gift items, toys, sports equipment, and home furnishings. Ads covered the latest arrivals, and the "Little Things Noticed on a Walk Through the Store" page kept readers au courant about unusual items for sale at Field's. The annual Christmas issue illustrated and described in detail everything from dolls for the girls and racing sleds for the boys to exotic glassware and china. Rene Mansfield of the advertising department served as the original editor; Clara P. Wilson was the first art director. The magazine was generally published four to six times a year; it ceased publication in 1978.

The cover of the 1921 issue of *Fashions of the Hour* notes that it is a 50-year remembrance of the Great Chicago Fire. Sketches from the spring 1933 issue of *Fashions of the Hour* show three copies of Paris originals: a Chanel coat (left), for $49.75; a Mainbocher ensemble of coat and matching dress (center), for $55.00; and an afternoon coat by Redfern, for $45.00.

CHICAGO FIRE
SEMI-CENTENNIAL
1921

FASHIONS
OF · THE · HOUR

MARSHALL FIELD
AND COMPANY
CHICAGO

1871

PLAIDS

THE plaid's the thing this year, from neckties to top-coats. It's a good thing, too, because you men have been letting your clothes get just a little uninteresting. And while it's a far cry from the brilliant tartans of the Highlanders to these modified and conservative patterns, there's a spirit about them that is distinctly new.

A sturdy windbreaker of plaid is lined with chamois and closed with a zipper. Light tan. 38 to 44. $20. Gray flannel slacks. $10.

Sports coat of Harris tweed. Bi-swing back, half belt. Tan or gray. 38 to 44. $18.50. The new slacks are of plaid flannel. Gray or tan. $8.50.

A definitely new idea is a well-blocked hat of light but durable fabric in a discreet Glen plaid with a stitched brim. Tan or gray. $5.

A gay plaid tie of heavy silk is a smart spring note, and will brighten up your wardrobe considerably. In various color combinations. $1.

The popular Glen plaid shirt with a tie to match will lend a refreshingly new appearance to any suit. 14 to 17. Gray, blue, brown. $2.50.

An English drape suit, beautifully tailored, has a fitted vest, lower button not to button, and pleated trousers. Gray plaid. 36 to 44. $55.

Clothes and accessories from the Store for Men.

A bright new version of the invaluable flannel robe has a wide scarf sash. Blue or maroon Glen plaid. Small, medium, large. $13.50.

These extremely good looking and well tailored plaid pajamas have the popular convertible collar. Gray, blue, brown. 15 to 18. $3.50.

Author's collection

THE MEN'S STORE

Marshall Field and Company's business saw tremendous growth throughout the 1880s and 1890s, necessitating larger quarters. The store kept expanding with new buildings to meet the demands of its retailing services; in 1914, Field's constructed a twenty-one-story building at the corner of Washington and Wabash Streets. One day at the State Street store, president John Shedd was in an elevator crammed full of shoppers. A lone gentleman was puffing away on a cigar, and the ladies were of course coughing. Shedd called for a staff meeting, at which he exclaimed, "I've made up my mind to get the men out of the store! We'll put all the men's departments in the new building." This he did. Floors seven through twenty-one comprised rental space. On the sixth floor was the luxurious Men's Grill, decorated like a men's club, with marble floors, dark mahogany furniture, and a fountain and a Favrile glass domed skylight by Louis Comfort Tiffany. The Grill was known for serving hearty food and being a welcoming retreat, where a man could have a smoke, eat a steak, and take a refreshing break from his work—or conduct business if so desired. The Grill could seat 750 and had seven party rooms and twenty-one booths; it was dismantled during the 1970s. The first five floors became the Marshall Field's Store for Men, featuring exclusive men's fashions and accoutrements and connected to the State Street store by an underground tunnel. Although Field's was geared toward women's wear, *Fashions of the Hour* magazine never failed to include a prominent ad for the Store for Men in each issue.

The 1930s window display of men's formal fashions echoes the era's Art Deco influence.

Marshall Field's Archives

The Pink Boutique features fashions from British shirtmaker Thomas Pink; the shirts are internationally renowned for luxurious fabrics, cut, and finish. The boutique opened in 2002.

The 28 Shop was created in 1941; it was renovated in 2001 to make it more browser-friendly.

THE 28 SHOP

Most renowned of the Marshall Field and Company departments is the famous oval-shaped 28 Shop on the sixth floor. In 1941, Field's was the first department store in the world to establish a designer shop "within a shop." When it was built, the 28 Shop—named for the entrance at 28 East Washington Street as well as the number of its rooms—was the epitome of elegance. Joseph Platt, who had created the sets for the movie *Gone with the Wind*, developed the concept for the shop. He devised a series of twenty-eight individual rooms encircling a central salon. The result was a designer dress shop that rivaled the best that Paris had to offer. Among the early designers represented were Hattie Carnegie, Adrian, Norman Norell, and Omar Kiam.

The 28 Shop held its formal opening on the evening of September 30, 1941, in a ceremony that matched the splendor of a Hollywood premiere as searchlights swept the skies, police on motorcycles kept traffic moving, guests from among the elite of the Midwest appeared, and thousands of spectators lined the sidewalks, taking it all in.

During the heyday of the 28 Shop in the 1940s, each room featured an exotic theme, and designs ranged from lace on the ceiling to bamboo on the walls. From the shop you could place a phone call, have lunch served on the department's own Lenox service, or write a note on 28 Shop stationery. In 2001 the 28 Shop underwent its most recent renovation. Today it is still known for carrying the cream of the crop from American and European designers.

Today's clean, elegant, modern look for the 28 Shop.

THE LEGEND CONTINUES

In 1952, as Marshall Field and Company celebrated its 100-year anniversary, a fourth grade teacher asked her students to define the store in just one complete sentence. A boy said, "Marshall Field's is where Santa Claus stays when he comes to town." Another boy added, "Marshall Field's is a place where they've got everything good in the world and it's miles high and miles long, and always jammed with people." A shy girl in the back of the room got up slowly, blushed a bit, and stammered, "Marshall Field's is . . . well, it's Marshall Field's, that's what it is!" And how right she was; the store is unique, a trendsetter, an ultimate destination for shoppers. The little things we take for granted—the restaurant in the department store, the bridal registry, the ability to return a purchase, the opportunity for a woman to shop and dine unescorted—these and many more innovations were pioneered at Field's.

But the store is not sitting on its laurels, not by a long shot. In 2003, the home store located at State Street underwent a massive renovation. It now offers 800,000 square feet of retail space to shop in, with 16,000 square feet devoted to shoes alone. Hidden staircases and antique chandeliers were uncovered and displayed. New "hot zones" throughout the store feature the best-of-the-best merchandise. The Bridal Salon showcases top-of-the-line designers, including Vera Wang, Marisa, Watters & Watters, Romona Keveza, Reem Acra, and Toni Federici; the Atelier Aimée features Italian couture bridal fashion. Among the big-name designers are Oscar de la Renta, Marc Jacobs, and Badgley Mischka; Field's has exclusive rights to

Thomas Pink in the United States, along with other brands. The latest names include Diesel, Paper Denim & Cloth, Burberry's, and a host of others.

Marshall Field's continues to uphold its cooking and food traditions. The store carries fine spirits, cigars, and gourmet foods and chocolates and holds wine tastings. The Culinary Council helps to identify the latest culinary trends and brings outstanding food and cooking ideas to the shopper. The venerable Walnut Room entices those who appreciate fine dining. Field's complimentary personal shopping extends the store's famed customer service, helping shoppers to update their wardrobes or create a new look and to select gifts. Events for the customers are ongoing, from a flower show to a flea market to the Glamorama fashion show to the 2005 Jacqueline Kennedy: The White House Years exhibition which highlighted the former first lady's gowns, dresses, suits, and accessories within a historical context. The Marshall Field's Archives await you on the seventh floor; there you can view gems from the store's past, including old perfume bottles, women's shoes, fashions, and promotional posters.

Marshall Field himself set the course for superb food and fashion; today the store pays homage to his legacy. "The Marshall Field and Company Idea" (see p. 64) still prevails, and will as long as good quality and service are appreciated. Field's exemplifies retail at its best.

Marshall Field's Archives

In 2003, Field's took center stage with the country's first vertical fashion show. The front of the store became the actual runway for a unique event. Specially trained athletes and models from Germany were suspended on cables and modeled fashions while walking, dancing, and "flying" down the facade of Marshall Field's on State Street. Crowds of people watched as Field's once again proved its understanding of retail as drama.

"The MARSHALL FIELD & COMPANY IDEA"

TO DO the right thing at the right time, in the right way; to do some things better than they were ever done before; to eliminate errors; to know both sides of the question; to be courteous; to be an example; to work for love of the work; to anticipate requirements; to develop resources; to recognize no impediments; to master circumstances; to act from reason rather than rule; to be satisfied with nothing short of perfection.